D0768414

My Perfect Son Has Cerebral Palsy

By

Marie Kennedy

Marie A. Kennedy, author
Tracy E. Brown, editor
Stephanee Killen, editor

ISBN: 0-75960-954-3

This book is printed on acid free paper.

Direct questions or comments to:
Marie Kennedy@aol.com

1stBooks – rev. 2/16/01

About the Book

This book shares the thoughts, concerns, and unrelenting faith of a young mother whose son, Jimmy, was born with Cerebral Palsy.

Jimmy -- a bright, exuberant, and loving child whose smile, makes you want to smile, just happens to have Cerebral Palsy.

Jimmy's mother, Marie, believes in a common sense, hands-on approach. She promotes bonding with doctors and therapists and utilizing innovative therapy techniques to enhance Jimmy's physical and emotional well being. She lovingly details what it is like, on a daily basis, to be a caregiver for a child with Cerebral Palsy. In sharing her creative ideas, utilizing inexpensive techniques, to enhance Jimmy's physical comfort and emotional well being with the cumbersome braces, she motivates and inspires.

By encouraging other parents, with special needs children, to ask questions and become fully informed, she removes the reticence they may feel to confront the matter directly. Further, she inspires the parent to avoid being shy about getting fully engaged in their child's treatment, and to listen to their fundamental instincts as to what is best for their child. This approach creates a feeling of positive activism for both parent and child alike, as opposed to tentativeness or indecision -- which can emotionally stifle both parent and child in resolution of the child's special needs.

This book is a tender look at not only a mother's frustrations and fears, but also of her dedication and triumphs, in a collective determination of spirit, with her very special child. We are empathetic and engaged with her as she overcomes all obstacles to become fully knowledgeable about Cerebral Palsy, and then become fully engaged with her child, as she comforts and encourages him every step of the way. The depth of her compassion, and Jimmy's positive reactions, encourage and stimulate the reader to embrace this overall integrated approach.

She shares her thoughts about the special bonds of family members -- the sheer joy of Jimmy's accomplishments, one step at a time -- and the heartbreak of having to handle the comments and stares of those outside the family circle. The interrelationship of all these factors serves to emphasize the importance of each; and the mother's ability to set the tone for parents, the extended family and friends, and the child. In so doing, the tone is also set for the child's outlook for the future, and his or her relationship in the world at large.

Marie Kennedy's writing style will both enthrall and stimulate you, by giving you a unique insight into her daily life. You will be inspired, as well as motivated, by sharing this in-depth look at the special bond she and her husband Chooch share, in giving to Jimmy an optimistic and realistic blueprint, for a full, happy life and a bright future.

You will laugh, you will cry, you will be raised to great expectations for the possibilities of life in the face of adversity as you share one woman's enduring odyssey with her child. From her joy at the birth of her precious child, to the unrelenting challenges of daily life that confront both parent and child, you will be left with both a full heart, and a renewed sense of wonderment at how we can all rise above adversity and achieve miracles, through dedication, determination, and of course, unconditional love.

I try not to think, "Why me?" I think, "Why not me?" Would I rather it be my brother, sister, stranger, or friend? We will do whatever it takes to raise our son to be happy, strong, and confident. This book was written from my heart, as a story of love.

There are approximately 50,000 children a year diagnosed with cerebral palsy. Every child and situation is different. This is a story of love, patience, encouragement, and advice from a mother with a child that has cerebral palsy. My hope is that some of this information will help you too.

W hen we were told that our only child had cerebral palsy, we felt helpless. This book is our story and includes some of the things we have done to help our son and ourselves. We are very happily married and I am lucky enough to be able to stay at home. My age, attitude, and patience have enabled me to spend a lot of time and energy helping our son.

My name is Marie, I am thirty-five, my husband James (nicknamed "Chooch" in high school because his football coach said that he ran like a train) is forty-six, and our son, Jimmy, is two years old. I am not a doctor or therapist.

This book describes some of the things we thought of to help us deal with walkers, crutches, braces and the possibility of a wheelchair. I will share some of our personal stories and advice on things you may be able to do at home. My purpose in writing this is to provide a resource of non-medical information, like that which I wish I could have found after Jimmy was diagnosed.

I married my best friend on October 9, 1993. We spent two weeks in Jamaica in January 1994, and I had hoped to get pregnant then. I knew this was the man that I would share the rest of my life with and that Chooch would make a wonderful father. Becoming parents was a dream we shared. By February, we had purchased two home pregnancy test kits, both with negative results. In early March, I went to see the doctor and had a blood test taken. We both waited anxiously for the phone to ring. Then, on March 15, at 10:30am, the phone rang and I received the excellent news. I had the nurse repeat it twice. Chooch and I laughed, cried, and danced all over the house.

Saint Patrick's Day was just two days away and my family always gets together for the parade downtown (my maiden name is Murphy). We decided to hand out Happy St. Patrick's Day cards to our family addressed to Grandma, Grandpa, Aunt, and Uncle. We signed them Chooch, Marie, and Baby on the way. Everyone was excited and happy for us.

I had some difficulty during my pregnancy with high blood pressure and needed bed rest and diet control. Chooch went with me to almost all of my appointments and my Mom came along on a few too. We heard our baby's heartbeat and saw our precious child during the ultrasound. We attended birthing classes, which we really listened to—being sure to participate and pay close attention. We were asked if we wanted to be tested to see if our baby had Down's Syndrome, but we weren't sure if a test like that would matter to us. I remember my Mom looking at me with tears in her eyes and saying, "Don't do it. They are *all* God's children. Everything will be fine." We didn't have the test done.

We began to get the baby's room ready and waited with increasing excitement. Although this was our first child and a new and scary experience, I was happy everyday. At night, I would rub my belly and say out loud, "Your Mommy and Daddy love you and we can't wait for you to be born."

Sometimes, I think he heard us talk to him because on Chooch's birthday, September 22, I went into labor. We were going out to lunch to celebrate his birthday and I felt odd—odd enough to stop at the doctor's office on the way. I felt sure she would say, "You're fine. You have two more months to go." She didn't. What she did say was that the baby had dropped; she could feel the head and I had started dilating. I burst into tears. I knew it was just too early. She

2

told Chooch to get me carefully to the car and drive directly to the hospital. She called ahead so they would be prepared for us. Chooch was so excited that the baby might come on his birthday, but the doctor said, "Hopefully not, it's too soon."

I spent eight days in the hospital on medication that would prevent contractions. Chooch, who is an entertainer, would come to spend the night with me after he finished his gigs and had to sleep on a foldout chair bed that threw his back out. On the eighth night, my water broke and the doctor said I could deliver our baby. Chooch was in the middle of a song when his beeper went off. He arrived at the hospital before I had been taken to the delivery room. We called our families and my parents came immediately, along with my brother and one of my sisters. (The attending nurse said that I could have someone else help along with my husband because of his back and I asked my mom.) My mom has delivered five children and never got a chance to watch their delivery.

There were a few complications, but we were excited because we didn't know the sex of the baby yet. The very moment he was born, my husband's back stopped hurting. He nearly skipped out of the room to tell everyone, "It's a boy!" We had discussed several names but decided on James Blair Kennedy III, after his father and grandfather.

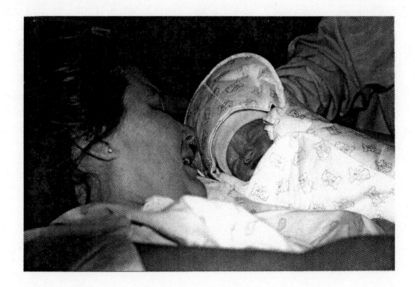

So, on September 30, 1994, we became the proud parents of a 4 lb. 10 oz. perfect little boy. Jimmy was almost two months early and had to stay in the hospital for eight days. We knew we would have to learn to use a heart apnea monitor before we could take him home and we were both a little afraid. Actually, I was more than a little afraid. I was scared to dress, feed, or hold him—he was so tiny. We had to take baby CPR classes, "just in case." My mom took the course too. It took all of my strength to listen, participate, and understand. I couldn't believe there was a chance that he might stop breathing or that his heart might stop beating. The little dolls they used to teach CPR were much bigger than Jimmy—and they weren't him. When my turn came to practice on the doll, I couldn't help but think, this could be Jimmy and I *have* to know how to save him. I did it, but I shook and cried afterwards.

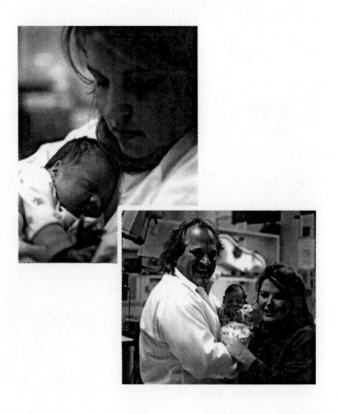

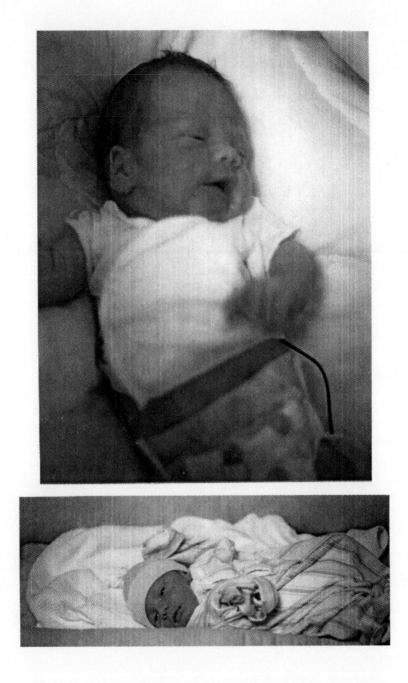

Although we had a dresser full of baby clothes, Jimmy was so tiny that none of them fit him; so we went to a specialty store that carried clothes for premature babies. This was also where we bought his first teddy bear, "Oatmeal." We brought Jimmy home on October 9th, our first wedding anniversary. What a precious gift for both of us.

A celebration with our families was awaiting us when we arrived. We laid Jimmy down in a little cradle my nieces and nephew had used and we set up a table next to it to put the monitor on. You couldn't help but watch the red lights blink. Talk about an alarm! The monitor went off in the middle of the night a few months after we had it. Chooch and I both sat straight up and jumped to his bed. Jimmy was okay; it turned out to be a bad cord connection. The monitor went off several times after that, but Jimmy never needed CPR. Looking back, I can't believe how strong we became in such a short amount of time, learning to use a monitor and to trust ourselves to take care of our child. I would pray every night to fall asleep with the assurance that if Jimmy needed me, I would know it and wake up. Giving back the monitor was as frightening as getting it. Now, we would no longer have an alarm although we were told that Jimmy didn't need it, he was doing fine.

Chooch was able to be home with me during the day and we had a lot of family and friends come to visit and help. One day in particular sticks out in my mind. It was one of the first times I was all alone with Jimmy. He woke up and smiled at me. I fed, held, and rocked him. He went back to sleep and began to hum. The sound was very soft and soothing. It was the same sound I used to make when I was pregnant and couldn't sleep. I would rub my stomach and hum, almost a moan, until I finally fell asleep. Having Jimmy make this same sound gave me confidence and my fears disappeared. I knew that we were connected and that I would do anything I had to do to help him grow up to be happy and strong. After that day, I looked forward to time alone with him.

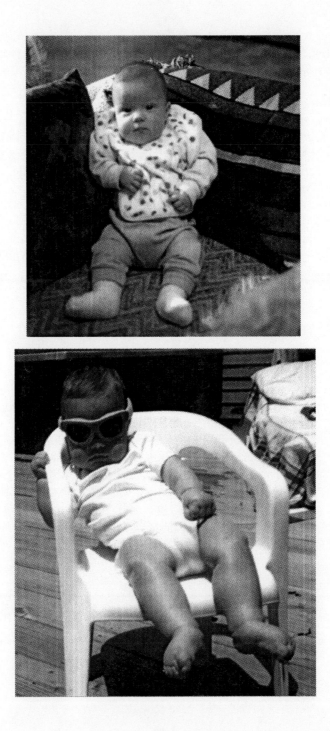

From the first day we brought Jimmy home, I kept a baby book/journal on what he ate, drank, his BM's, who came to visit, and what we did everyday. I also kept track of his movements, his illnesses, and the results of his regular check-ups. I wrote down the questions I asked and the answers I received. We also had a nurse come by our house while Jimmy was on the monitor about once a month, for six months. Everyone thought or said that Jimmy was progressing and that any delays were because he had been born prematurely.

Jimmy started saying Mom and Dad from about six months old and was always happy and good-natured. However, by Jimmy's first birthday party, he still wasn't sitting up. I could prop him up with a pillow or put him in a highchair, but he seemed to be very uncomfortable. He would lay on the floor and roll in the direction he wanted to go. At about fourteen months old, he began to army crawl on elbows and toes very low to the ground.

I remember being at my parent's house and my dad having tears in his eyes as he watched Jimmy get around. The next day, I asked my mom about it and she suggested that I take Jimmy to a different doctor. I agreed and felt confident that he would say that everything was fine, that Jimmy was very bright and was simply learning movement a little slower. The doctor that my mom and I took him to had been my doctor when I was younger and was still my parent's doctor, so I could trust what he said.

After looking at Jimmy's feet and legs and using a tone fork to check his hearing, he said that Jimmy had spastic tendons and suggested that we see a neurologist. I burst into tears and said, "I thought for sure you would say everything is perfect." He gave us the name of a doctor he said he would go to if it were *his* son, and that we would probably have to do stretching exercises. I went out to the car, hugged my mom and cried; so did she, although neither of us knew anything about what he had just said nor thought it odd that he'd referred us to a neurologist.

I went home and told my husband. He seemed to handle the news very well and said, "Let's wait and see what the specialist has to say and whatever it is, it will be okay." Our appointment with the pediatric neurologist was about six weeks later; we couldn't get in any sooner.

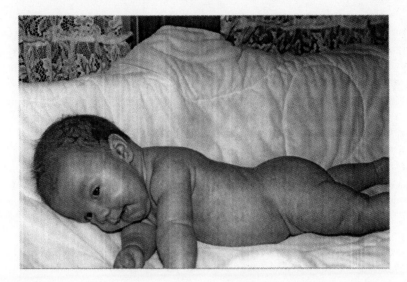

My mom and Chooch met Jimmy and I at the office. We were all a little nervous, but had no idea that the doctor would tell us what he did. He looked at Jimmy's feet and legs and tested his reflex ability. He tapped Jimmy's head and listened. He then kissed Jimmy, looked up, and said, "I am 99.9% sure that Jimmy has Cerebral Palsy." In a matter of about five minutes, our lives were changed forever.

We all stared at the doctor for a moment and then he asked me what I was thinking. Did I know what it was? My answer was no, but that when I heard those words I pictured crippled, retarded, and wheelchair bound. He explained that cerebral palsy would not get worse and that there are mild and severe cases. He said that Jimmy was toward the mild side. He also told us that we needed to get an MRI in order for him to be 100% sure.

He gave Jimmy to Chooch and told us that Jimmy would probably walk, maybe not normally, but he felt he *would* walk. Chooch asked if Jimmy would be able to play golf and he said probably, but that it was hard to tell so soon. He suggested we wait for the results of the MRI and then talk to a physiatrist (a doctor specializing in the evaluation and treatment of physical impairments). He gave us a number to call at a local hospital that had a cerebral palsy clinic. He looked at me and said that it was all right to cry, which I did after I could breathe again. He left us alone in the office for a moment.

December 15th is a day I will always remember. We had all driven separately and met at the office, so we hugged and cried in the parking lot before driving home. I do not remember driving to or walking in the door of our home with our sweet baby, Jimmy.

Jimmy had fallen asleep for a nap and Chooch and I stood in the kitchen not talking or moving. Moments passed before I finally said, "He's the same baby we walked in the office with as when we walked out." Chooch was holding onto the .1% chance that the doctor was wrong. He said he would carry Jimmy the rest of his life if he had to. Whatever it was, we would do everything we could to help.

We began to wonder if this cerebral palsy was due to something we had done in the past to ourselves or to someone else. Then, the phone rang, it was the neurologist calling to see if we had any questions. This was my opportunity to ask the question on our minds, "Was it our fault?" No, he told us. Cerebral palsy is caused during pregnancy or birth and is not hereditary. Many times, the reason for it is never known. I thanked him for calling and then the waiting began. We couldn't get in to see the specialist for another two months. We wondered what we were supposed to do now. We had a lot of questions without answers and I wasn't sure where to look for them.

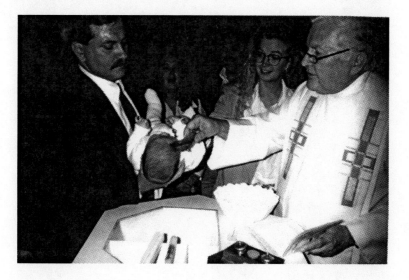

We knew we had to tell the rest of our family; they all knew about the appointment. My mom was able to contact my sister-in-law, Dianna, and told her over the phone. My dad was at their house sitting at the kitchen table and could tell by Dianna's face and her tears that it wasn't good news. He began to cry before he even knew. My mom also called my brother, Marty (Jimmy's Godfather) and asked him to tell my sisters, Helen (Baby) and Angie in person, since they work in the same office building. Marty went to see Baby and asked her to take a break and come outside. He told her what he knew. "Jimmy has cerebral palsy." She told me that she'd cried, but Marty never did—he seemed to be almost angry. When she returned to her office, she called her fiancé, Joe. Marty then went to tell Angie. She cried and later told me that she'd wanted to hug him, but he was so rigid she thought he might have broken down if she had. Marty has three healthy children of his own and I'm sure he was thinking, "It's just not fair." My sister Tracy (Jimmy's Godmother) lives out of town. I called to tell her and her fiancé, Larry who was there with her. I was able to remain calm as I told her; I really amazed myself.

Chooch had called his mom, Beba, and told her; they both cried. I can't explain how hard it is tell your parents and family news such as this because your

heart is breaking and you're telling them news that will break theirs too. Beba called Chooch's sister Corya and her husband Lee, who lived out of town. Chooch called his dad and whatever was said seemed to calm him a bit. I called Chooch's brother John and talked to his girlfriend, Leesa; John was working late. During our conversation Leesa said, "Well, some of your dreams for him may change." I told her, "I don't think so. My dream for him is to be with a woman that he loves and for her to love him back, like I do his daddy. He should be able to attend regular schools. I hope he makes good decisions on his career and other personal choices and follows his own dreams. Cerebral palsy shouldn't stop that." Leesa had given me something to think about, but the answer came right off the top of my head and I still believe it today—even more.

John called me when he got home. Chooch had gone to sing at a wedding reception. I couldn't help but feel for him—being in a party atmosphere and having to sing. There was no time to find a replacement and he couldn't cancel at the last minute. I asked John to go downtown and be with him. When John arrived, it was late and Chooch was almost finished, but he was thankful for the love and support. John's only son Derek was working out of town at the time and received a call from John regarding the news. He later sent us a note of support.

I am so thankful for all the people who told someone for us. Just saying the words made me get a lump in my throat. That was a very emotionally draining day, but the more it was said, the easier it got. It was important to share our information and feelings every step of the way because early on, we'd decided that shame and embarrassment was never going to be a part of Jimmy's C.P. I started calling aunts, uncles, and friends and telling them what little information I knew. After we talked to Marty and Dianna, we decided to wait to tell their children: Ryan, seven; Amanda, five; and Lauren, two. All three are just crazy about Jimmy and love him so much; we knew that they would be full of questions we didn't have the answers to yet and how upset they would be.

Everyone that had not talked directly to Chooch or to me began to come over or call the next day. They all offered love, prayer, and support. Many of our friends and relatives told us of other people they knew that have cerebral palsy. Some of them are still children and some are adults, but all have accomplished many things and with some, *you can't even really tell*. I hear this a lot. Chooch has a second cousin with cerebral palsy, a more severe case than Jimmy. They are not very close, but Chooch told me what little he knew. Months later, I called and talked to her. We had a lovely conversation and when I hung up the phone, my heart was full of hope, love, and respect.

I seemed to do better on the phone than in person, as far as controlling my emotions. Many people called and I reminded them that Jimmy had been on a heart apnea monitor for six months and we had all lived through that. I also emphasized that his condition would not get worse and that it was not going to kill him. If he needed extra help learning to walk, so what? We would help him. The only thing that had changed was that we now knew why he hadn't been sitting or crawling. We just needed to be patient and find out more.

Going to sleep that night was hopeless. The words **CEREBRAL PALSY** swirled in my head in very large letters and echoed in my ears. Jimmy was sleeping fine, but I had an urge to pick him up, to hold him and kiss him and tell him that everything would be all right. But he was fine. *I* was the one that needed to be all right. I knew I had to get the strength to function and the next morning, I was on a mission. I called United Cerebral Palsy, ordered a book from them and asked them to mail me any information they had.

My parents came over the next morning. I had not talked to my dad yet. We have a special connection that enables him to look at me, know that something is wrong, and usually make it better. This was something that he could not fix. Walking in the door, we were both fine, as long as we didn't really look at each other. I took his coat as he came in, and I saw the hurt in his eyes. I broke down and cried with him; we hugged for a long time. My dad is the strongest man I know. He wants to take your pain away. Jimmy considers my dad his buddy and even calls him Bud instead of Grandpa. They have a special connection too. Dad not only felt for Jimmy, but for us. He loves and respects us and he knew we were afraid.

Within half an hour of being around Jimmy laughing, doing tricks, and giving hugs and kisses, we all felt better. John came over too. He looked around and saw Jimmy, then picked him up, hugging him tightly. I could tell that he was about to cry when he said, "The last thing this little guy needs is pity. He's so bright and strong, he's going to be fine." Just watching Jimmy look into his big blue eyes and seeing his smile and how happy he was, made everyone feel better.

News like this affects the whole family and whatever the reaction is, try to accept it. You can't control how someone will feel or act and whatever it is may be normal for them. I did ask everyone to try not to cry around Jimmy, he is very aware and I didn't want him to think that he'd done something wrong. So all my sisters appeared strong when they came over or when we talked on the phone. They just called each other and cried. Our families are full of love and emotion—we feel blessed.

Chooch seemed to be on hold until we were 100% sure. He can build and fix almost anything and did so in order to keep busy. I also tried to keep myself busy. We didn't talk as much as we usually did, but seemed to function fine otherwise. The house was clean, the laundry was done; Jimmy was happy and eating and sleeping well. Chooch spent a little more time in his studio. I am not sure what he was doing; playing the guitar, listening to a new song, or maybe building something. Music is an outlet for him. He sings from the heart and you can see it in his eyes. We usually talk about everything, but what do you say when you're both trying to be the strong one? We said I love you a lot.

A few days had passed when John stopped by. I asked him to watch Jimmy while I took a shower. Once in the shower, I realized I hadn't taken one in four days. I tried to drive to the store and felt like I was in a video game, so I turned around and came back home. I think I was in a state of shock. I was aware of it and didn't drive until I felt like I could. I had cried at first, but then wouldn't allow myself to cry, worry, or be scared and upset all the time. I was afraid that if I ever really cried, I wouldn't stop. But one morning, almost a week after we heard the news, I went downstairs and laid on the living room floor. I cried, kicked my feet and moaned. I just couldn't seem to let it all out. Chooch came downstairs and held me. I cried and whispered, "My heart is breaking, my heart is breaking." It physically felt like something was squeezing my heart.

That day, I decided that I needed to grow up and be strong for myself and for my baby. I try not to think, why me? I think, why not me? I am full of love and patience and I am a wonderful mother who will do whatever it takes to raise our baby to be happy, strong, and confident. I thought of all the times I'd seen other babies and parents with a child that was retarded or physically handicapped and I'd felt sorry and wondered, "how do they do it?" It always made me feel better if the parents seemed to really love the child. I felt that they were all blessed. *God doesn't give you more than you can handle.* I heard this a lot, too.

I am not sure where my strength comes from. It could be either the love and support of my family, faith, or angels watching over me; maybe a combination of all these things. I *do* know that you need a special strength and I believe that everyone has it. Find your strength and use it.

Along with strength, you need knowledge. Ask questions, read, and call organizations to request information. Try not to be overwhelmed by information that does not apply to your child.

In a few short weeks, cerebral palsy stopped being two huge words swirling in my head and became two little words in a book. The MRI test was scheduled for December 27, 1995 at 9:30 a.m., so we had to be there at 8:00 a.m. We were awake and nervous by 6:00 because we knew Jimmy would have to be sedated during the process. This was one of the few occasions that Chooch seemed to need me.

Chooch appeared to be fine and soothed my fears up until he had to hand Jimmy to a nurse and leave the room. Feeling helpless, we walked away to get a soda and wait. I was holding Chooch's hand when I looked up and saw that he had tears running down his face. He held me tightly as he cried. I trust doctors and tests a little more readily than Chooch. I told him that sometimes, you just have to trust and reassured him that they seemed to be very careful and loving.

The time dragged on and on. A few hours later, they came to get us and said that everything went fine; Jimmy was awake and drinking juice. We knew that he had finished earlier, but we couldn't hold him until he was awake. We walked in and when he smiled at us, we knew he was fine. More questions arose as we waited for the results. I was nervous during this period. I kept wondering, "If it isn't C.P., then what is it?"

The neurologists called on January 3, 1996, and confirmed that Jimmy did indeed have cerebral palsy. He said that it had occurred before birth and that it was like a little scar around the ventricle of his brain. There are various types of C.P., but hypertonia spastic diplegia is what Jimmy has. This means that the muscles in his legs have high tone, or are pulled tight all the time. Now, we knew the type and had a definite diagnosis, but still didn't know what we could do. I continued to rub lotion on his feet and legs. I had done this every night since we brought him home, but now I did it a little longer and tried to rub in my love, faith, and hope that his little legs would someday work like everyone else's. Even today, after every bubble bath, he says, "Lotion massage." I smile so much that some days my face hurts.

Our next appointment was with the physiatrist, but was set for February 28, 1996, so we still had several weeks to wait. I called and asked if Jimmy could be tested in advance. I had read that before any treatment was given, a child had to be evaluated.

We were able to schedule a physical/occupational therapy test for January 26, 1996. I felt very protective of Jimmy all that morning because I didn't know what they would do to him. I felt like it was an us/they situation. After we met the therapists doing the evaluations and discovered that they were warm and friendly, my guard slowly came down and I was able to ask the questions I wanted to and honestly answer questions from them. They didn't have all the answers, but assured me that the physiatrist would.

Jimmy had just begun to try to pull up and stand at home and was really trying hard to move around. The physical therapist suggested that we order leg braces right away, from the knee down, and start therapy twice a week. She said that Jimmy might need a walker, too. The occupational therapist said that Jimmy did not need this type of therapy right now. The speech therapist suggested that he see her once a week. He had been talking from six months old, but wouldn't talk to her during the testing.

Marie Kennedy

Jimmy seemed to be having fun with all the toys and attention. We had pushed him in on a little bike with a handle, his feet, up on a footrest. He loved the long halls of the clinic and would wave to people and blow kisses on the way in and out. I had a very good feeling about the help that he would receive. A social worker talked to us about a federally and locally supported program that would pay for all the therapy he would need until he was three years old: *The First Steps Program*. This was a big relief financially. We would have come up with any money needed, but it was nice to know that we didn't have to. We also found out that our insurance would cover his equipment. We were very fortunate.

There are foundations, federal and local, that you can apply to for assistance. If you do not have insurance or an income to pay for the equipment your child needs, they will help you get it. If you don't know who or where to call, look up social services and call them, or ask your doctor.

I was determined to be strong and do whatever we needed to do. I called everyone again and told them the results of the evaluations and about how good Jimmy had been during all of it. I also talked to Dianna again and told her that the kids should know since Jimmy would have braces soon. I didn't want them to be afraid to play with him. Marty and Dianna told Ryan and Amanda that night. (Lauren was too little to understand.) They told them in a simple way that the children would comprehend. Both Ryan and Amanda cried and asked questions. Amanda had wanted to take Jimmy to show and tell on his bike the week before and wondered if she still could. Ryan called his Grandpa in Maryland and asked him to get on his computer and send all the information he could find on cerebral palsy. They both went to school that Monday and asked for all of the kids in their class to pray for Jimmy everyday. I have found, not just with Jimmy's cousins, but with every child that we have met, that it is much better to tell them in a way that is simple: "Jimmy has cerebral palsy, he needs a little extra help walking." They have questions and sometimes tell me of other people they know that may use a walker or wear braces. They usually want to hug Jimmy and that is fine with me. He is a love bug.

Jimmy was only sixteen months old when he began therapy and from his first session, he worked hard the entire hour, even on the days he was sleepy or crying. He was starting to use muscles in a way that he never had before and some of it was physically painful. In the beginning, I didn't talk very much. I watched Jimmy and his therapist. I watched how she held him, worked his muscles, and seemed to control his movements. I watched other mothers with their children and therapists.

Sometimes, the child would cooperate better when the parent wasn't in the same room. After a couple of sessions, I started asking questions and having the therapist show me what she was doing so I could do it at home. I made notes and she printed out instructions with pictures explaining how to stretch Jimmy's legs and strengthen his back muscles; some of which I had been doing already. I believe that a mother knows, almost feels, her baby's pain. I had good days and not so good days. Sometimes, I would have to leave the room crying. Watching your child try so hard to do the things that are so easy and everyday for most people, touches your heart. I made friends with the executive secretary, whom I am thankful for. If she saw tears in my eyes, she would hug me and offer encouragement. She always reminded me of how well Jimmy was doing. After talking for a few minutes and splashing water on my face, I felt better and could go right back in.

Chooch came to therapy when he could, and his mom, Beba, has attended also. All of my sisters came at least once. My parents have been there the most. It can be hard to watch. Sometimes, it is harder for me when I have a family member to look at, or see the tears in their eyes. This is when you need to accept whatever someone can give. My sister, Angie comes to our house at least once a week and is wonderful with Jimmy, but it is hard for her to watch Jimmy at therapy. My dad told me that he might not be able to come to therapy anymore because it broke his heart. There are times when Jimmy cries, "Help me, Mom!" I want to grab him, run out the door and not come back. I know that his therapist is not hurting him and that he needs the therapy. On bad days, we take a break and I hold him, talk to him, and ask him to try again. He does and always gives hugs and says thanks before we leave.

Jimmy was fitted for his first pair of braces. The braces are made at a separate place near the clinic. I had an odd feeling all morning, as if the back of my head were numb. I was so nervous going in for the fitting that my hands shook while I was looking for our insurance card. I took several deep breaths and told myself, "Calm down." We waited for a few minutes and someone called

Jimmy's name. We went into a little room and I took Jimmy's shoes off and rolled up his pants. The orthotist (professional that makes the casts) was warm and friendly. He sang a children's song while he rolled the wet plaster on Jimmy's legs. I had to hold Jimmy down and try to soothe him at the same time. It only took about five minutes, but seemed like half an hour. We left after the fitting and scheduled a time to pick up Jimmy's new "shoes." He kind of liked them. I was relieved that they didn't seem to hurt him. They were lightweight, all white plastic, and attached with Velcro strips. I was so proud of Jimmy for accepting the braces and letting me put them on without a struggle. I was also glad that my mom came with us, but I still cried driving home from therapy while Jimmy was asleep in the car. There were times when I wondered, "How am I supposed to feel?"

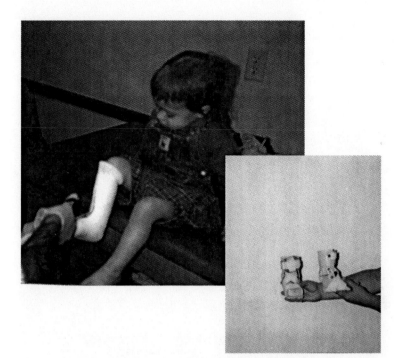

Chooch and I decided to go out to dinner with Jimmy to celebrate his braces. This was the first time we noticed other people looking at him. While waiting for our table, we held Jimmy. His pants came up and you could see his braces. I know people can't help but look, but I wasn't ready for it. Although part of me wanted to leave, we stayed and went to the table. The few times we went out in the past, we'd put him in the standard wooden high chair most restaurants have. We put a jacket behind him so he could lean, which lessens the strain on his hamstrings. We didn't realize that putting him in the chair with braces would take practice. It seemed like everyone in the room was staring. My ears became red and I had a lump in my throat; my heart was pounding. We finally got him into the chair. It took both of us. I held him under his arms as Chooch guided his feet through the small leg holes. The waitress took our order and Jimmy started to cry. He was very uncomfortable and so was I. I asked Chooch if we could just leave. He found the waitress and we gathered our things and went home. I felt like a big baby later, but realized that I needed the time to adjust. I didn't want to push myself to do everything as usual. Everything was not "usual." I wasn't embarrassed; I felt protective. I wanted to yell at them, "What are you looking at!" I'm glad I didn't.

The next time we tried to go out, I was prepared for looks and stares. I smiled and took my time putting Jimmy in his seat. I gradually became more comfortable and we go out often now. For the greater part, I liked the braces,

27

too. For Jimmy's sake, we all liked them and told him that they were cool. We said hi and bye and hugged the braces almost everyday. I knew that no matter what I felt inside, Jimmy needed to know that the "shoes" were a good thing.

Jimmy started new things almost immediately. He began wearing the braces on February 12, 1996, and started standing for a few seconds at a time by February 17, 1996. He was also progressing in speech therapy. I watched through a two-way mirror. His speech therapist explained to me that although his C.P. is in his legs, it affected many other areas as well. Jimmy wasn't crawling yet and he was sixteen months old. His back muscles needed to be developed and with that, would come stronger and louder speech.

I was learning something almost everyday about C.P. and about myself. As I told you in the beginning, I have kept a journal on Jimmy and what we do everyday. I am not going to tell you what happened in every therapy session, but he was progressing quickly. I want to tell you some of the landmark days for me.

On February 19, 1996, Jimmy took his first steps! (18 months.) He was standing and holding onto a little wooden table and moved his feet, just like anybody else, and took steps. We met Chooch, Baby, Angie, and Marty for lunch; everyone was so excited. I am calling them steps, but it was more like what an eight-month-old would do along a table or couch. However, it was a whole lot more than Jimmy had done before. My heart was full and I cried off and on all day, calling everyone to tell them the news. I can't explain how much relief I felt from those few little steps. He certainly was not walking on his own, but his legs and feet *could*. That's what I prayed to see. (I pray everyday and have since I can remember.) I had not been to church after finding out that Jimmy had C.P. I was a little afraid that I would break down.

Ash Wednesday was February 21, 1996. Jimmy had therapy and the chapel in the clinic was having mass. I went in and sat in the back. I looked around the room and thought of all the different reasons why people were attending mass in the hospital. Some were workers, many were not. I knelt down to pray and started to cry. I couldn't stop. It felt like I opened a door that I'd kept shut because of my anger, fear, and confusion. I continued to cry throughout the mass, but left feeling light-hearted and less afraid. I went to get Jimmy from his therapist and she told me that she would be fitting him for a walker soon. He had tried one that they had and it scared him. She said that this was normal. As Jimmy slept on the way home, I cried some more and told myself not to be upset, that the walker would help him.

Finally, our appointment date arrived—February 28, 1996. This was the doctor who would answer our specific questions regarding Jimmy's condition. She would also plan his rehabilitation program, such as the amount and type of therapy, the equipment he would need, etc. To say I was disappointed would be an understatement. I am not going to go into detail, but I felt belittled, rushed, and defensive. There was a definite personality conflict between the physiatrist and myself. My mom and Chooch were also upset at the way she'd treated me. Except for telling us that he needed night braces, she gave us very little new information. I felt as if I had wasted my time filling out all of the forms sent to us in the mail prior to the appointment. After thinking about it and talking to several people, including my mom, I decided to talk to the social worker and see if it was possible to get Jimmy assigned to a different doctor. She agreed, a new doctor was assigned, and an appointment was scheduled for four months later. In the meantime, Jimmy continued therapy and we ordered braces for Jimmy to sleep in.

Requesting a new doctor wasn't an easy thing for me to decide. After talking to my mom, I thought of all the times she'd protected me and stood by my side. I realized that I needed to do this for Jimmy. If I have a bad pair of shoes or a meal in a restaurant prepared wrong, I return them. This was my baby and I needed to be able to communicate with his doctor and feel good about it.

The reason I told this part of my story is because you will have to make a lot of decisions and need to be comfortable enough with the person giving you the options to ask questions and to truly understand. Don't be afraid to say, "I don't understand, could you explain this again? Could you draw a picture? What are the risks?" Get a second opinion and/or doctor if you're not happy with who you have. You're not just taking your baby to get his shots, you're helping plan his therapy, which will determine his abilities.

Jimmy's therapy was scheduled for midmorning, so I always brought along a snack for him. In addition to that, I always had his blanky with me for the times when he needed comforting. If your child doesn't have a blanky, you might bring along a favorite toy or treat. I may not always have candy with me, but I always have a hug. Jimmy has come to count on that as much as I do.

As Jimmy became more able, he wanted to do more. I noticed that when he would try to carry things and dropped them, he would become very upset. I began to say, "So what? If we have a big mess, we just clean it up." Now he laughs and says, "So what," and helps me clean it up.

Try to understand your child's frustration and acknowledge it. It seems to soothe Jimmy when I say, "I know, I know" as I hug him. He began to say this along with me too.

* * *

You can and should be a part of your child's daily therapy.

Here are some of the activities Jimmy enjoys doing that serve as therapy at home. We added games and toys as his ability to use and play with them increased. Please consult your child's therapist and/or specialist before attempting any of these. **I am not qualified to advise on what activities your**

child should be doing, but these are examples of what has worked for Jimmy.

Stretching Jimmy and putting his braces on are as much of our morning routine as brushing his teeth. The following are what we do every morning:

- I usually lay Jimmy on his dressing table, or we both sit or lay on the floor. I rub the bottoms of his feet, tickling and patting them. (His feet are very sensitive because his braces cover his feet and his shoes are worn over that, so his feet do not touch the ground often.)

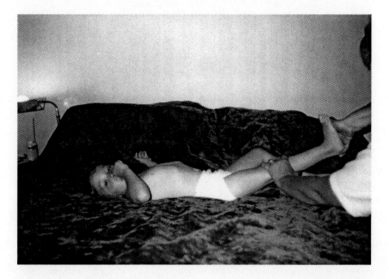

- After the massage, I ask him to relax (he pretends to snore, like his Daddy). To stretch his calf muscles, I hold his heel firmly and press his toes towards him. At the same time, I hold his other leg still. I can physically feel his cords stretching as I monitor his expression to decide how far to go. We count from one up to fifteen, depending on the type of day he is having.

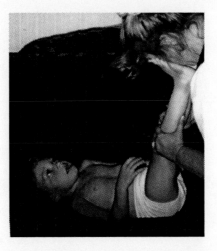

- I noticed that stretching his hamstrings was painful; Jimmy kicked in resistance. I had to find a way to do it, so I put the balls of his feet on my eyes, knowing that he would not kick me. Once his feet are on my eyes, I push his legs towards his belly and hold for a few seconds. I then gradually stretch them straight up. Throughout this exercise, his feet remain on my eyes and I am able to move my head forward while securing his knees and hips with my hands. We repeat this eight to ten times.

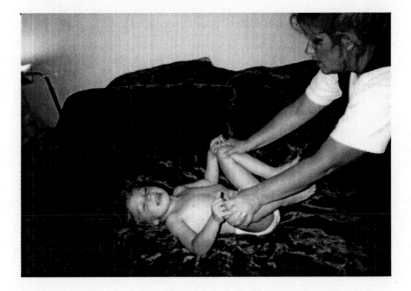

- To help his hip and inner thigh muscles, I push his legs back, almost up against his stomach. Holding on to each knee, one at a time, I rotate them in a clockwise motion. We sing the ABC song for each leg, keeping his mind off of the stretching while teaching him the alphabet.

I asked his therapist if he was in pain. She suggested an activity that would give me an idea of how his legs might feel. She told me to bend my arm at the elbow, in towards me, and hold it until it shakes. After seconds, my arm began to cramp. I then released my arm and held it out straight. I could feel the tension in my muscles. I also stretched myself at home, similar to the stretches that I do with Jimmy. I wanted to have an idea of how it feels for him and I needed a better understanding of what actions cause what muscles to move. I also asked his therapist to observe the way I stretched him in order to make sure that I was doing it correctly. Again, I feel it is imperative to have a comfortable, open relationship with the therapist. One of the reasons that it is so important to ask before trying something new, is that children with spastic tendons can get pulled muscles very easily. A pulled muscle can inhibit their progress until it heals.

Jimmy had only been in therapy for three months and his hard work already seemed to be paying off. One night, I took Jimmy out of his highchair and put the top half (the chair consists of two large plastic parts, which can be used both as a table and toddler chair) on the floor and Jimmy stood up, held onto the back of the chair and walked. Chooch was home and he and Jimmy had the same look on their faces. We stayed close to him to keep the chair from going forward too fast. Jimmy was walking! I wanted to call everyone, but we would see most of the family the next day at my parents for spaghetti. We decided to surprise them. We brought Jimmy's highchair and placed it on the floor and he walked,

pushing the chair all over the living room. The whole family clapped and hooted and some jumped up and down. They also had tears in their eyes and turned away so that Jimmy wouldn't see them cry. I looked around the room and I didn't see my dad. He had gone to a sink to soak his head and push his hair back, I guess to keep from boo-hoo crying. When he came back to the room, we all laughed and said, "Oh, Jimmy won't notice that."

In the next therapy session, Jimmy was fitted for night braces and a walker. While driving home, I could feel the tension in my arms and shoulders as I looked at Easter decorations and thought, "Jimmy can't go egg hunting. He will have to watch other children having fun." Tears ran down my face until we were home.

We picked up the night shoes on March 11, 1996. They looked like little ski boots. One was green and the other was orange. (Jimmy got to choose the colors.) I wondered if Jimmy could sleep in them. Part of me wanted to throw them out the window. I thought, "Why can't he sleep in comfort?" They didn't seem to bother him and he slept in them all night from the first night we picked them up. The Velcro straps stuck to the blanket and he would become tangled up, so I put socks over them and they were fine.

After a few nights, I realized that it was bothering me more than him. I had to quit being selfish and thinking of the things he couldn't do and start concentrating on the things he could do.

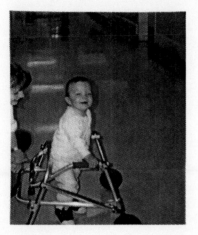

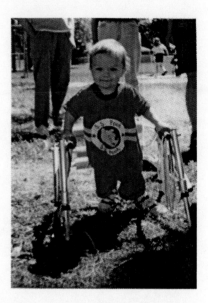

The braces were working and his walker arrived on March 14, 1996. He had been using one at therapy, but this one we would bring home. The walker goes behind him and he pulls it along to help him keep his balance. It is similar to the ones that older people use, but it is pulled from behind instead of pushed from the front. This method helps him to stand up straight instead of leaning forward.

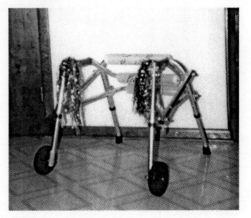

On March 17th, we went to visit everyone to show off. Jimmy could go almost anywhere with his walker. He was so determined and loved the independence he had with it. He loves applause and he got plenty of it. That night I thought, "Two years ago today, we announced I was pregnant and what a happy day it was. Today, I am filled with just as much happiness, love, and pride." I decorated his walker with bicycle streamers on the front rubber grips and bicycle pads on the back three bars. I took his walker into a bicycle shop and asked them to help me. The pads I used were the type that attach to the center bar of a bicycle for protection. I bought an extra set for the walker he used at therapy. His walker looked so cool that other kids wanted one. The pads also helped protect his teeth and face if he fell trying to pull himself up.

I began to work more and more with Jimmy at home. I watched him move and began to think of things that we could alter to help him be more independent. One idea came to mind because Jimmy had also begun to crawl for the first time. We needed to get him on his hands and knees and actually move his legs for him. After much repetition at home and in therapy, the muscles in his back became stronger and he was able to crawl very well and fast, though he still could not stand alone or keep his balance for more than a few seconds. One day, I was doing dishes and heard Jimmy say, "Here my come, Momma," but his movement sounded very slow. I looked around the corner and saw him with one of my slippers in one hand, trying to crawl to bring it to me. I wanted to go pick him up and get it myself, but he was so proud of himself. I went back to the sink and let him bring it to me. He gave me a kiss and went back to get the other one. It sounds like such a simple thing to do, but it's not for Jimmy.

One day, I found a blue and red plastic three tiered cart with wheels. When we came home, I took all but the bottom basket off and Chooch secured the lid on top. It looked a little like a mailbox. The best part was that Jimmy could now put things in the basket and push it with his hands while up on his knees. This was a good exercise for him and was fun. I also found a little wooden chair that needed a lot of work, but the size was perfect. Jimmy sits more comfortably when his knees are bent. The muscles in his hamstrings are so tight that he can't sit on the floor or in a chair that forces his legs straight out for more than a few moments.

Chooch took the chair a few days later and put wood strips along the bottom, almost like a rocker, but flat, not curved. He reinforced all the strips, painted it, and then covered the little seat to match our dining room chairs. It fit perfectly up to his table cart. The strips on the bottom prevent it from tipping over when Jimmy pulls himself up or turns to sit. He uses it everyday and looks so proud of himself when he can do things on his own.

I bought a few more carts and put toys in them so that he could reach them himself. We began to play games where we would take everything out and then put it back. Reaching and bending exercises are more fun this way and easier on me emotionally if I can make them enjoyable. We play kissing games on the steps. Chooch and Jimmy put on little rails to match the big ones so that he could go up the steps by himself. When he is too tired, he crawls and we kiss between the wood strips, more stretching and balance work, and a game we both enjoy a lot.

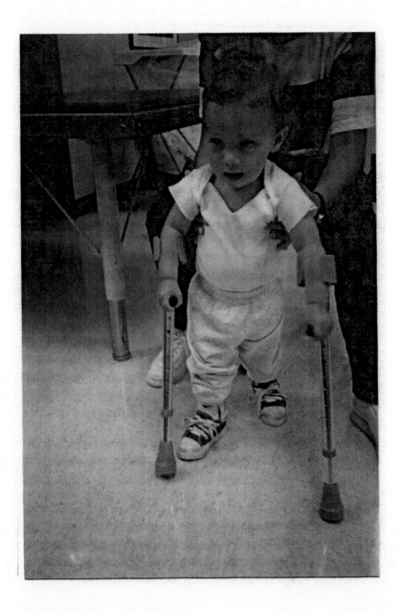

Jimmy was doing so well that his therapist decided to try crutches at his session on April 16, 1996. He did not love them and neither did I. For some reason, the walker seemed easier to accept. (I almost told to myself out loud, "These little crutches are one step closer to Jimmy walking on his own.") I knew from what little experience we had that our reaction would definitely affect his. At therapy, even if we didn't use the crutches we said, "Hi and bye," to them and I said, "I love these crutches. They are our helpers." Jimmy started to like them too. We ordered him a set for home on May 15, 1996. (20 months old.)

Jimmy was also working on sitting up. It was such a struggle for him. His sweet face would get red while he pushed hard with his arms. It was heart wrenching to watch him work so hard to do things that younger children do without thought. Within a month, he was sitting up without help. It was still a struggle, but, "By myself mama." To hear him say this and see the twinkle in his eyes made any other feeling fade away. He was learning something new almost every day. (I have been putting the dates in to illustrate how quickly he learned and progressed.)

A few other things had started to happen. He was standing alone for a few seconds at a time and looked so anxious to just take a step, but he was cautious too. Jimmy also had to learn to fall. The tendency he had was to fall back like a tree and hit his head, or forward hard on his knees.

As his balance got better, he would be able to fall better and less often. I wanted to protect his knees, yet keep his mobility, so I purchased several different colored terrycloth wristbands for adults that fit his knees nicely. These were inexpensive and machine washable.

The crutches came in a month later and we brought them home. I was full of mixed emotions. The pads they had given to me at therapy were sticking to his skin. I remembered the terrycloth seatbelt pads for his car seat and thought they would fit perfectly. I made two cuts on either side and folded them over. They have Velcro fasteners that keep them secured to the crutches, come in various colors, and are machine washable.

Being able to make him more comfortable eased me a little, but I still had days where I wished that he didn't need the extra help and thought that maybe I always would. Chooch knows when I am having one of those days or when something is difficult for me and we talk to and encourage each other. I find that if we don't talk when I feel sad, then I feel guilty. I don't have time for guilt or room in my heart for it, but I am human and expect to feel many different ways as Jimmy and the whole family grows from this experience.

Two days after we brought the crutches home, Jimmy walked, holding onto one of his therapist's hands. This was the first time that his balance was good enough. He saw himself in a mirror, smiled big, and said, "Hello, Jimmy." We all clapped and cried. Even now, we try to celebrate each accomplishment. It is an unbelievable feeling when your hopes and dreams come true right before your eyes.

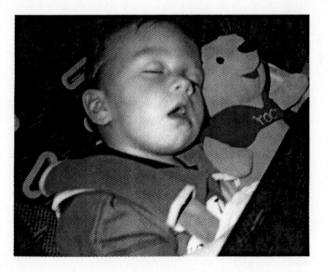

A few days later, Chooch was swinging Jimmy; he always pushes higher than I would and they both love it. (Sometimes, I have to go inside because I am so protective of him. Chooch takes chances with him that I would not.) That same day, Jimmy crawled in the grass for the first time and had a blast. He actually came in the house with grass stains on his knees. This was the first time I needed to pre-treat his pants before washing them. I cried doing laundry because I felt such a relief that maybe he really *could* play and do the things that other children do. I always try to be positive, but don't want to be disappointed or expect too much. I want to be able to accept what he cannot do and what we cannot fix.

That summer was fun for all of us. Jimmy loved the pool and playing outside. Chooch has played golf since he was seven years old and had his first hole in one on Father's Day. Jimmy almost jumped when he came home and told us. Jimmy has a little set of clubs and leans against the couch and swings them. He told his dad that he would play when he gets bigger. We believe he will.

The appointment with the new physiatrist went well; we liked her. She listened to me and answered all of my questions. She also acknowledged Jimmy's accomplishments, which was important to us. She told us that we might need to think about surgery on Jimmy's left foot when he gets bigger. The braces were working on correcting the way it turned in, but he may need corrective shoes when he is fully-grown. We also talked about a wheelchair. Jimmy was walking, but tired easily. He would soon be too big for a stroller and too heavy to carry. She suggested that we wait another six months. She believed that he would walk on his own by this time. Although the appointment was easier with our new doctor, we left with a lot of mixed feelings. I'd really hoped she would say that he would not need a wheelchair, but she didn't. She *had* said that he may walk without help and that was exciting to think about.

Jimmy also had an appointment with his neurologist. He looked at Jimmy and the reports of his progress and said, "I will always be Jimmy's doctor, but, I don't need to see him again. He is doing great." We couldn't help but notice a mother with her daughter making her next appointment. She was about Jimmy's age when he was first diagnosed and she looked like I felt after our first appointment when we found out that Jimmy has cerebral palsy. She was by herself and I wanted so much to hug her and tell her to be strong and to love her little girl—that there was hope. I also wanted to tell her about all the progress Jimmy had made with therapy and equipment. I don't know how I would have felt if a stranger hugged me and told me these things, so I didn't say anything. After we went into the doctor's office, I didn't have to. The doctor asked us if he could introduce Jimmy to her and show her how well he was doing and how happy he was. Of course, we thought it was a great idea. After this appointment,

I didn't feel sick to my stomach every time I drove by his office. This appointment was all good news.

Winnie the Pooh was Jimmy's favorite video and he loved Tigger, too. We found out that they would be at a nearby mall. Jimmy and I went to the mall a lot to use his crutches and walk. We made some friends and it was always fun to see the joy on the faces of strangers watching him walk and seeing how happy he was. He spoke to everyone and checked out the store windows. I didn't know how Jimmy would do in a crowd when Pooh and Tigger were there. My sister Angie went with us and the line was longer than any Santa line I had ever seen. I brought Jimmy's walker because it was easier for him than his crutches.

Children and parents were getting anxious for their turn and the line was moving quickly. Jimmy wanted to walk up by himself. Part of me wanted to carry him because I didn't want all those people staring at him. Then, I looked at his sweet face and thought, I don't care how long it takes, he can do it by himself. He did. He walked right up to Pooh and gave him a big hug. Luckily for us, they were going to switch to Tigger and he got to hug him too. He was so happy he looked like he would pop. Everyone was looking at him; some with sad faces, which make me the most uneasy, but most of them had big smiles on their face after seeing his.

Therapy, August 7th (23 months old), was such a happy day. Jimmy's therapist was holding his hips and getting him to balance and stand up straight. She looked at me and let go and then Jimmy took three perfect little steps without help. Wahoo!! I wish everyone could have seen it. I couldn't get the smile off my face; it hurt by the end of the day. I wanted to hold out my arms and spin in circles like a little girl, so I did. We called the family and I cried off and on all day.

Jimmy would continue to try to walk by himself at therapy, but not at home. Almost two months later, Jimmy walked at home without crutches between Angie and me. We would help him get his balance and then let go and he would walk back and forth. Chooch still had not seen him take steps alone, but Jimmy walked to his daddy on Chooch's birthday, September 22, 1996. We were having a party at our house and he walked to everybody. This was the first time that my nieces and nephew saw him walk, too. Amanda jumped up off the couch and yelled, "Yeah, Jimmy! Walk to me!" More tears and applause. Jimmy loved it. I know I already mentioned the love and support of our family, but I love so much to share the happy times and to see the happy tears and hope in the eyes of those we love.

The next birthday was Jimmy's, September 30, 1996. Two years old, wahoo! We had a big party at our house for him. Chooch found a battery-powered jeep for Jimmy to drive, but needed to make some adjustments to it first. He did and Jimmy loved it. He drove all over the yard as I held my breath in the hopes that he would not get hurt. He wore a helmet and Chooch was always right next to the car, able to physically stop it if he had to.

I calmed down and watched them together with a happy heart. He was really proud of himself and so happy. He had recently learned to sing happy birthday and did, very loudly. I asked everyone at the party to write a note to Jimmy in my journal. The messages were so sweet and heartfelt. It was a day of reflection for me on how far he had come over the past months and of how determined we

all were, but mostly, I thought of Jimmers. After he went to bed that night, I was talking with Chooch when I decided to write this book. I wanted to share my ideas and feelings with others and let them know that they are not alone. I feel that I have a special child in so many ways and it is easier for me to write down my thoughts than to speak them aloud. There are so many things you can do that no one ever tells you.

As I mentioned before, one thing that Jimmy and I liked to do was go to the shopping mall and walk. We went three to four times a week. We would start on one end and when we made it to the other, Jimmy would get a balloon. We stopped along the way to rest and to look into shops. Although Jimmy had begun to walk without assistance, he still used his crutches to build endurance.

One day, there was a "most photogenic" contest at the mall and we entered Jimmy in the category of "most beautiful." He wore a tuxedo and stood with his crutches for the photos. The prizes were awarded a month later at the mall. Jimmy won the people's choice most beautiful 2-3 year-olds award. Wahoo! We won the negatives and, the best part, a trophy. My mom, Angie, and Beba came with us and were all so excited. Hundreds of children had entered and the photo we picked to enter was a face shot. Jimmy's picture was like the others. I was not ashamed of the pictures we had taken with the crutches, but I didn't want someone to vote for him because they felt sorry for him. Jimmy said, "I won, I won, Mama!" He smiled big and held his trophy up as everyone clapped. Of course, there were tears along with the smiles and laughter. We are all a little emotional.

As happy as that moment was, an incident a few days later would bring us to the other end of the scale. Jimmy and I were at the mall and had just said hello to Santa; he knew Jimmy by name. I noticed an older woman, late sixties or early seventies, with two children about six and eight and another woman who I'm guessing was her daughter-in-law. We were walking towards each other, Jimmy, on his crutches, when I saw her turn the heads of the children so that they would not see Jimmy. The mother of the children just watched. As we came closer to each other the older woman said very loudly, "She should keep him at home." I knew that she'd meant for me to hear and for a second, my head was numb. I felt like a cat, arched with the hair on the back of my neck standing up. Several people stopped shopping and looked at all of us. Jimmy and I just stood there for a moment.

The older woman was taller than I was, but I looked right at her. I moved closer to her and spoke calmly when I said, "Who do you think you are? We have every right to be here. He is not ugly, offensive, or contagious. He has cerebral palsy and has worked hard to get around as well as he does. I am not embarrassed or ashamed and hope he never is, even though there are people like you that say ignorant things like what you just said. Happy Thanksgiving!" She didn't say a word, but had tears in her eyes. Jimmy had fallen down while standing next to me, so I helped him up and we walked away. I could feel everyone around us watching. I swallowed the lump in my throat and we kept going to the other end to get our balloon.

When we came home, I almost didn't tell Chooch. It was much harder to re-tell than to react when it happened. I was used to people looking and giving a pitiful smile, but I never had anyone say something offensive out loud. I told Chooch and then cried as he held me and told me how proud he was of Jimmy and me, but that it may happen again. We both agreed that I'd handled it well, without crying or getting mad and yelling. I have found that I don't mind answering questions. I would rather someone ask than to stare. I realized that this older woman grew up in a different time, but hiding handicapped children was wrong then, too. I respect my elders and felt a little funny that I had brought her to tears, but I didn't do it, she did. You need to speak up when you feel it is necessary and ignore what you can. Someone is bound to say or do something mean and how you handle it will reflect on how well your child does when he deals with things on his own.

I have talked to Jimmy about the braces, walkers, and crutches. He is very aware that not everyone uses them. We talk openly about cerebral palsy in front of him because I have never considered it something to whisper about. He needs to know that his equipment enables him to do the new things he is learning to do. He thinks that his braces, walker, and crutches are cool and that we love them. That is a stretch, but it helps all of us.

On Thanksgiving Day, my dad asked about what happened at the mall in front of everyone. I couldn't finish the story, so Chooch did. Later, my nephew Ryan, who was sitting next to me said, "I knew it would happen, I just didn't know when. I feel proud, not any other way." He had just turned nine years old and had been worried about Jimmy. I assured him that we were both fine and that sometimes you need to stand up for yourself. I started crying because it had hurt me to hear someone say such things and it was hard for me to repeat it. He understood and gave me a hug. We all continued to have a great day and realized again that talking and sharing experiences and thoughts helped all of us.

Jimmy was gaining confidence in his ability to walk. He no longer needed someone to hold his hands and get him started. He was also falling better, becoming less cautious, and growing more anxious to try new things.

We went to Florida on a vacation and had a lot of fun together. He crawled almost the entire time, maybe because it was a new place. I encouraged him to use his crutches, but he didn't want to. Although he was over two years old, we didn't discourage him from crawling because it strengthens his back muscles and shoulders.

He had worked so hard those past few months; he was now standing, squatting, and getting up without falling. On October 24, 1996, he let go of a table, turned and walked, not just steps, but walked. Wahoo! We began calling Jimmy, Big Boy U.S.A.

By the middle of November, he was taking sixty steps at a time without any help. He could stop and keep his balance and start walking again.

In January of '97, Jimmy and I went to the school my niece and nephew attended and visited the classrooms. I talked about C.P. and brought his walker and crutches. All of the children were interested and asked a few questions, mainly, "Does it hurt him?" I explained that his muscles were very tight and on some days, his legs were sore, but that we were doing all we could to help him. We thanked them for their prayers and they drew Jimmy pictures and hugged him good-bye. It was a fun day for all of us.

A few months earlier, I had met Sandy. Her son Joey has C.P. as well. Joey is about a year older than Jimmy and his brother Eric is a year younger. Sandy and I became fast friends; sharing ideas and letting our children play together. They lived very near to us and we encouraged each other. Jimmy and Joey helped each other, too. Joey was still using crutches and Jimmy was using his less and less. Joey could ride a bike everywhere and Jimmy couldn't at all. They watched and learned from each other. I hoped that they would stay friends.

I was able talk to Sandy about the day I threw Jimmy's braces and shoes across the room and left crying. Jimmy picked them up and threw them too. That is the day Jimmy learned the word, aggravated. Chooch and I are both calm-natured. I explained to Jimmy that, "Sometimes, Mommy has a bad day too. I was wrong to throw things and I am sorry." Sandy understood the aggravation of buying shoes that would fit over the braces and socks that come up high enough for the braces, but are thin enough too. We celebrated each other's accomplishments and shared our fears of what was next.

Sandy also told me of Joey's physiatrist. She told us that he was very positive and we were anxious to see him. We made an appointment and I had prepared a list of questions. The main one was, "Will Jimmy need a wheelchair?" He said, "No," without hesitation, "not now anyway." Jimmy had begun to take steps when his braces were off, though he was still up on his toes and his feet were turned in. The doctor was impressed with his achievements and encouraged us to keep doing what we were doing. Chooch liked him the best of all our doctors, but our insurance would not allow us to see him regularly. We wanted to continue to take Jimmy to see him along with his other physiatrist. We hoped to see him twice a year.

He encouraged me to let Jimmy play and walk sometimes without his braces and to let him kick and splash in the pool. He told me not to be so concerned all of the time about how he sits and moves, but to let him be a little boy. He also told us an Indian proverb: "Once you've mounted an elephant, you will not fear the bark of a dog."

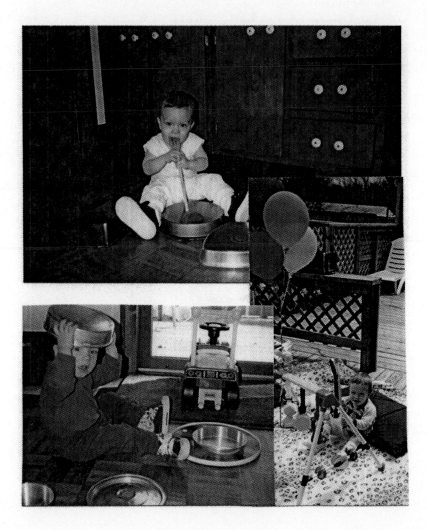

*   *   *

Special children should do special things whenever possible. Here are examples of some of the things we do at home. I have included these to show how a little imagination can go a long way.

The following are examples of daily activities and games.

- Sitting with legs outstretched is a good stretch, but not very comfortable. We get around this by placing bowls or pans in front and to the sides of him and giving him spoons. The noise and action takes his mind away from any discomfort.

- While on his knees, Jimmy has fun pushing bowls and pans around the room. This helps his hips and strengthens his back. (Try the kneepads.)

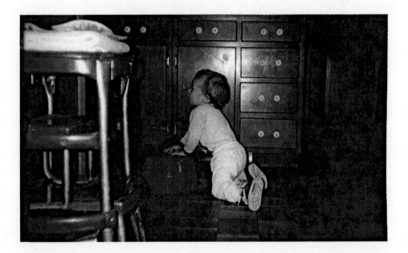

- I put decorative magnets up and down the legs of a metal chair. Jimmy takes them off one by one and puts them on the refrigerator. This is easier than asking him to bend and stand for no reason.

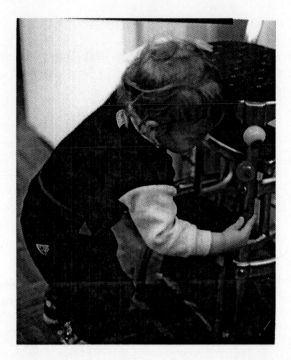

- We play a "surprise" game to get Jimmy to reach. I put small toys or candy under cups and Jimmy reaches from side to side, as well as forward, in order to find his surprise. This works well sitting or standing.

- Bubbles are a great tool for almost any type of movement. Jimmy will reach to catch or pop them. He will also extend his legs trying to step on them. This is good for weight shifting from one leg to another.

- We march around the house like a train taking turns blowing a train whistle. Getting Jimmy to lift his feet when he walks is so much easier this way.

- We put a small basketball goal on the living room door, attached with suction cups, which easily accommodates small foam balls. This activity is beneficial in a number of ways. It is great for stretching, weight shifting, and more importantly, it is a confidence booster. The basketball goal was moved to the big tub when Jimmy became strong enough to sit up on his own.

- Giving your baby a bath is always fun. Jimmy wasn't able to sit up in the big tub when he was younger, so he stayed in the little one with a sponge on the bottom. I stretched him while he was in there. I taught him to fill a little plastic bowl with water, and then lift and pour it on himself. This strengthens his back and arm muscles. It also helps with coordination.

- Jimmy loves to draw. We put a plastic art easel and chair outside where he can either sit or stand while creating works of art. Giving him the option to sit or stand allows him to play longer, while the repetition of this movement makes it a more natural transfer of positions, regardless of tight muscles.

- We hung a big beach ball from a string on the patio. It hangs just at Jimmy's eye level. Jimmy is learning to pass and catch the ball. He also uses a plastic bat to swing and "bamm" at it. He loves this and laughs every time he hits it. This game helps with balance, weight shifting, coordination, and confidence.

- Sitting on the floor is difficult for Jimmy. The way he wants to sit is like the letter M or W, which is not good for his hips. I couldn't tell him he was sitting the *wrong* way, so a therapist suggested that I ask Jimmy to sit a *different* way. When I do, he shifts to side-sitting. He has to use one of his arms to balance and hold himself up. This limits his activity. We use his little chair or let him use a gardening pad on the deck to kneel on when he is outside to color or play.

None of this has to be expensive. Eighty percent of Jimmy's toys were purchased at garage sales. Going to these sales also allowed us to meet our neighbors and talk about Jimmy. Someone would always ask, "Why does he wear braces?" I prefer this question to, "What's wrong with his legs?" Saying, "Jimmy has cerebral palsy," became easier the more I said it. It didn't matter that many did not know what it was, he captured their hearts in the few minutes that we were there. Most offered to keep him in their prayers, which we thanked them for.

One particular garage sale had a special bonus—pony rides. Wahoo! The woman who owned the pony told me of her son who has cerebral palsy as well. He is a teenager, living in a group home because he is a quadriplegic and needs constant professional care. She shared her experience with me and said, "Of all the tears I have shed, each accomplishment—big or small—has brought many more smiles." She takes comfort in knowing that his soul is whole.

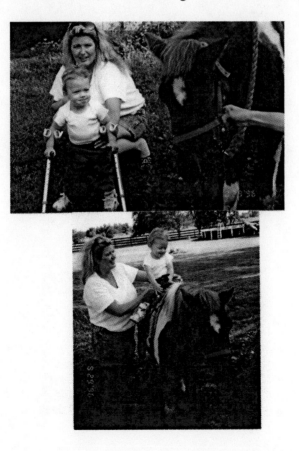

When buying toys or gifts, consider how your child can and should move. It can be disappointing to receive a gift and not be able to use it. Our family consults us first on birthdays and Christmas before making purchases, which helps to avoid this problem.

Jimmy is our only child, so we are able to give him many unique opportunities. He has been to a number of outdoor concerts, including some of Chooch's. He loves meeting the guys in the band and really enjoys being in large crowds. I bring his instruments with us and he plays along. He also has access to his Dad's real instruments out in our studio, which is where he can spend time with his dad while allowing me some time to myself.

It is necessary for both parents to take time out for themselves. Chooch helps me with many of the day-to-day tasks that can seem overwhelming when you try to do it all, but the truly important thing that he does is simply to be there for me. He comforts me when I worry about the small things and has a way of keeping things in perspective. I don't realize how much I worry until I stop. I tell myself to enjoy each day and not worry about the future. Like, "How will Jimmy walk when he is fully grown? Will his knees buckle in? If someone that walked a little funny asked me to a dance when I was in high school, would I have said yes? Will other kids make fun of him?" You can become overwhelmed with thoughts of what if? It is so very important to let others help you. If something is difficult for me to do alone, I ask someone to help. I have learned the difference between pity and help. Remember, this affects everyone that loves your child. I don't want people to look at Jimmy and feel sorry, I want them to look at him and see a little boy with challenges that he faces like a man. Jimmy is our hero. He wakes up with a smile on his face.

I had tried to go to church with Jimmy several times. (God has always been a big part of my life.) After attending a few times and going to communion, I noticed everyone looking at us. I have been Catholic all my life and know everyone watches people coming and going down the aisle. I am used to people looking at Jimmy's face and then looking down to see his braces, and their face changes as they look away. I see this at the store and when we go out to dinner, but seeing a hundred people on both sides of me as I carried Jimmy made me nervous and flushed and my knees got weak. I thought I would pass out. I quit going to church for a while and continued to pray at home, as I do everyday.

I was a new member of the parish and decided to make an appointment with one of the priests in order to tell him my feelings. It helped a little and I would continue to try to go to church, but more importantly, I have met some new friends and have been able to kneel down and thank God for all of His blessings. I do not pray that the C.P. goes away, I pray for us and for Jimmy to be able to accept his abilities and struggles, and continue to work and play hard to do any and everything Jimmy wants to do.

Marie Kennedy

By April of 1997 (2½ years old), Jimmy was walking everywhere. He was standing on his own and learning to walk up and down the steps. He was kicking a ball and trying to ride a bike. Chooch and I decided to throw a big party. I always wanted to have a party with his band playing; what better reason than Jimmy's independence? We decided to have the party on July 4th weekend; Sunday, July 6.

The next few months were filled with plans, calls, and doctor appointments. Jimmy has to go regularly to have his hips x-rayed. Sometimes, children with C.P. don't stand enough to create a deep enough hip socket for their legs and they pop out. The doctors keep a close watch on this. Jimmy also sometimes gets athlete's foot. His plastic braces cover his legs as well as the bottoms of his feet, and his night braces need thin socks inside and out of them. (I asked the men that make his braces to drill holes in them for air. This seems to help, along with changing his socks and washing his feet during the day when it is hot out.)

Jimmy almost always says his feet and legs are fine, when I know from stretching them that they are tight or blistered. He still walks or tries to and says, "I am okay, don't worry."

He had begun walking all the time, sometimes saying, "Go Jimmers." He is so proud of himself and should be. By May, he was trying to ride a tricycle and did with help and special pedals to keep his feet on. He had learned his A-B-C's and numbers 1–10. He was singing on a play microphone, playing the drums and the harmonica, and anything else Dad would let him. He knows the guys in the band and loves to watch and copy them.

Plans for the party were coming along fine. We expected one hundred people. On Father's Day, Chooch played golf and Jimmy and I slept in. When Jimmy woke up, he didn't want to walk and crawled to see Chooch when he came home. I can't explain the expression on his face when he tried to walk; I just don't want to see it again. He fell down and said, "Mom, I can't do it." I was panicked, but wouldn't show it. I held him and told him we would try again later.

I made an appointment to see his specialist the next day. She could not find any reason for him to stop walking. She had me get his braces adjusted but it didn't help. We waited another day; still no walking. We went back to see her again and she suggested that we take him to see his pediatrician. He had blood work done and x-rays but there was still no real answer as to why he'd quit walking. He kept trying to and would say, "See Mom, I am walking," maybe three to four pained steps. I called his therapist and asked her if she had any idea what it could be. She asked me to describe how he walked when he took a few steps. After I told her, she said she thought it was a pulled muscle and that he was limiting himself because it hurt. She explained how easy it was for him to pull a muscle when his braces are off and they had been, right before this happened. I could have pulled it while stretching him.

We waited a few more days and Jimmy gradually started walking like he had been before. Within a few more days, he walked in the yard without his walker for the first time. Uneven surfaces are difficult for him, so he uses the walker. He just left the walker and walked several feet before falling. He got right back up and kept trying.

As excited as we were, the big party did not change the reality that Jimmy still had C.P. We know that it is not going to go away and that there will be setbacks. There are several medical options as your child grows, including more braces and surgery. We have not had to make any decisions yet, but we are reading about our options and preparing to ask questions. We will deal with things as they come.

After months of preparation, July 6th finally arrived. Jimmy had tight hamstrings that day, making it difficult for him to walk, so we held his hand and had one of the happiest days ever. The weather was perfect. I saw cousins and friends I had not seen in years. Some of his doctors and therapists even joined our celebration. We had a clown come for the kids and they loved it.

Finally, the band was ready to play. I was anxious because I didn't think that I could thank everyone for their prayers, help, and sharing in our celebration without crying, but then Jimmy walked up to the microphone by himself and asked Chooch for it. When Chooch gave it to him, Jimmy said, "Thanks for coming to my party, I love you." I didn't need to say anything after that. Jimmy stayed near the band and sang *Knock on Wood* and *Soulman* with Chooch. He bobbed to the music of all of the other songs; he has great rhythm.

We decorated the yard with a banner that said, "Way to go Jimmy—Big Boy U.S.A." We hung windsocks and put red, white, and blue tablecloths on the tables. I had one white cotton tablecloth that I had everyone sign as a keepsake. We had a giant cake with flags, flowers, a rainbow, and balloons with "Walking by myself" on them. The bakery called the night before wanting to be sure that I wanted all of the things I had listed on the cake. I explained that it was what Jimmy wanted. They did a wonderful job and Jimmy's eyes lit up when he saw it.

The party lasted until almost dark. Angie was holding Jimmy when he said, "I don't want to have fun anymore, I just need my soft blanky." He thanked us before he fell asleep and said, "This was the best party I ever saw." Everyone had fun and we were thankful that so many loved ones and friends could celebrate with us.

The next day I was thinking about the party and remembered something that had happened a few months earlier. Jimmy and I had gone to the store. This particular store had a greeter that pulls your cart out for you. He noticed Jimmy's braces as I put him in the cart. He touched my hand and said, "God bless you, ma'am." I smiled and said, "He already did."

Update

It is important for me to tell you that Jimmy has cerebral palsy; it doesn't have him. He is pure joy. He is full of life and energy. He wakes up with a smile on his face and greets each day with anticipation. He is proud and excited for himself with each accomplishment. He is bright, funny, and sensitive. After his Aunt Angie told him, "Jimmy, you're walking so fast!" he said, "Thanks! I can walk slow, too." He also has amazing patience. He can eat finely shredded cheese one piece at a time.

Jimmy is accepting of himself and others. I can always count on him to help me through my bad days. He is a good boy that minds well, his eyes sparkle when he smiles, and he is generous with hugs and kisses.

It is now the fall of 1999. Jimmy is nearly five years old and is almost able to run. The past few years have been exciting for all of us; everyone celebrates each accomplishment. We have two new additions to our family. Helen (Baby) and Joe were blessed with a handsome, healthy son, Joey. He is almost two years old. Tracy and Larry were blessed with a beautiful, healthy daughter, Samantha. She is four months old. Jimmy loves to spend time with them and all of his cousins.

Jimmy started his third year of school and will attend five days a week, for two and a half-hours per day. He rides the school bus and has easily made friends. Jimmy is polite and charming, and always has something to say with a big smile. He is also very bright, asking questions and remembering the details of the answers. I knew he would ask me about his braces and I tried not to think about it. He also listens when I talk to others about him and cerebral palsy.

One day, shortly after Jimmy had turned four, he asked me, "Why do I wear braces?" I didn't hesitate to say, "Because they help you walk and play." He asked if his cousins Joey and Ryan would wear braces. I said no, that they didn't need them. I went on to tell him that his braces were cool, they have action figures on the back of them. He agreed that they were cool and started talking about something else. I didn't tell him more than he asked.

Marie Kennedy

A few months later, we were driving in the car and he asked, "Why do I have cerebral palsy?" He caught me off guard and my mind went blank. All the guilt and fear I thought I'd let go of came back and I almost burst into tears. I felt like I would rip my heart out and trade it in for a good answer. Finally, I said, "I don't know, honey. Some babies are just born with it and you're one of them. That's one of the many things Mommy loves about you." He asked, "Is cerebral palsy why I wear braces?" I said, "Yes, it is." He then asked, "What else do you love about me?" I began to list many things and we laughed about it. I later talked to my sisters individually about it and cried with them. They reassured me that my answers were fine and that it was understandably harder to discuss these issues with Jimmy than it was to discuss with strangers. Talking to Jimmy about cerebral palsy becomes easier the more we do it, but I let him decide when and what he wants to know.

He has learned to ride a bike and steers well enough to ride inside the house when it rains. We have found that a back on the seat helps his feet to stay on the pedals and to keep them going. He played baseball on a team and after only a few tries, was able to hit a ball pitched to him. The diamond was small gravel, which made it a little more difficult for him to go around the bases. Between third base and home, he was very tired. Another little boy from the other team drove up in his wheelchair and gave Jimmy a ride across home plate.

The next game was on a dirt field and Jimmy was excited to see it. He said, "Mother, I can run really fast on this one." He hit the ball again and went around the bases without any help. His grandparents were there to see him and he was very pleased with himself.

Jimmy has figured out a way to play or do anything that he has wanted to. We were watching a show where kids were skipping when I noticed that he was curious about it. I said that maybe he would skip when he got bigger. He watched for a few more seconds and said, "No, I don't think so—and I don't care." We both laughed.

He talks about being on a football and basketball team when he gets bigger. We tell him that it would be great, because we are confident we can find a team for Jimmy to be on if he wants to play.

Jimmy takes Tae Kwon Do lessons and is eager to show off his moves. The lessons are good for his self-confidence and balance.

At the age of five, Jimmy was certified with a White Belt, First Degree in Tae Kwon Do.

Jimmy is potty-trained. I have placed a bell in each bathroom to ring if he needs help. He can undress himself, although the first few times I watched him take his socks off were very difficult for me. As I've said before, what seems simple for most is a struggle for him, but the almost unbearable urge to help him is quickly diminished by the look of pride on his face when he is able to do things by himself. We still help Jimmy get dressed, but he picks out his own outfit and cologne for the day. (If you ask him, he'll tell you he has twenty girlfriends!)

Jimmy can walk without his braces. We found this out on a vacation in Florida. We went to Disney World and he insisted on walking all day instead of riding in a stroller. After a great day, we returned to our room where I discovered that he had quarter-sized welts on his legs. I knew that he would be unable to wear his braces, so I purchased shoes that fit his bare feet. Jimmy walked everywhere. He walked on the beach, in the grass, and he even played golf. After four days of no braces, he began to fall more frequently. He said what I already knew, "Mom, I need my braces."

Jimmy loves golf and spending time with his dad. They play miniature golf together and have been to a real golf course where Jimmy drove the cart and hit a few balls.

He caught his first fish, a blue gill. (Can you believe the size of that one?)

Jimmy loves computer games and is a whiz at them. He enjoys movies, cartoons, and sports on television. He will sit for hours with Chooch, cheering on his favorite team.

This summer, Jimmy was up on stage with Chooch at an outdoor concert. He sang, played air guitar and tambourine. He took his shirt off to pose like a muscle man and bowed after each song. When Chooch introduced him with the band, he very proudly said, "And this is my son, Jimmy!" The crowd went wild and Jimmy loved it. He clapped and blew kisses. I, of course, was crying. Driving home with Jimmy that night he said, "Mother, you can call me Chooch Junior."

We continue to work with Jimmy on a daily basis. He receives therapy once a week at school, as well as weekly home visits from therapists.

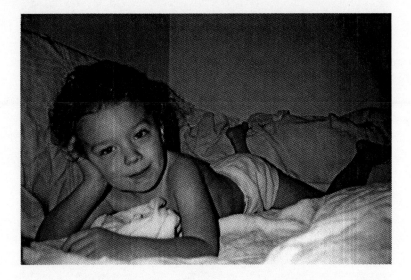

We are blessed and honored to be his parents.
Jimmy is the joy of our lives and perfect for us.
To Jimmers from Mom: Mama loves you every time, all the day.

Thank you for reading my book.

Marie Kennedy

This is the original version of the story I wrote published in *Chicken Soup for the Mothers Soul 2*

Jimmy's New Shoes

It is September 28th, two days before our sons 5th birthday. His name is Jimmy and he has a smile that lights up a room, sky blue eyes, and curly hair. My husband, Chooch (Jim), and I are taking him to buy a new pair of high top tennis shoes. We arrive at the store and look up and down the display of shoes. Dad finds a pair with the colors of Jimmy's favorite basketball team. He shows them to him and his eyes light up, "Lets try these, OK, Mother?" I look and find the style in his size and he sits down on a nearby stool. I have a lump in my throat as I take off the shoes he has on. I then remove the braces he has worn since his diagnosis of Cerebral Palsy at 16 mo. old. His therapist had recently talked to his specialist who agreed our pride and joy was doing so well, that we could try a pair of shoes without braces a few days a week. Jimmy was so excited to pick the pair he wanted. We are usually very limited in the selection that will fit over his braces.

I bend down, adjust his socks, and slip on the shoes. I lace them up and just as I finish the second bow, Jimmy jumps down and looks at himself in the mirror. He has his hands on his hips, like Superman. We are all three excited and I ask Jimmy to try and walk around and see how they feel. He takes a few steps and turns to see if we are watching. "Go on Honey," I tell him, "you're doing great." I am holding Chooch's hand and we both squeeze as we watch him walk faster and then almost run in his new shoes.

He has been walking at home without shoes or braces for months, but has had limited endurance. I am watching him march now with a great big smile on his face. I look at Chooch and ask, "How much are they?" We both laugh. "Who cares," he answered, "Jimmy is getting these shoes." I put his old shoes in the box and we pay for them.

He thanks us as we walk to the car. He is riding up front with Dad, clicking his feet and admiring his new shoes. I am quietly sitting in the back, thinking of all we have been through, especially our son, to get to this point. Jimmy is humming as we go inside the house. He wants to call everyone and tell them about his new shoes. I suggested we call just a few people and surprise the rest at his Birthday party. We have a large family that love and support Jimmy each step of the way. We make our calls and go through our nightly routine of warm bath, lotion massage, and a few stretches. I put his night braces on and kiss him good night. He again thanks me, saying, "Thank you for my new shoes. I love them, can I wear them to school tomorrow?" I assured him that he could. He fell fast asleep with his shoes right next to him on the bed.

As happy as I was, I was a little worried he wouldn't want to wear his braces again. The next morning, as I helped him dress for school, I talked to him about it. I explained that he could only wear his new shoes a few days a week. He said, "My braces are cool Mom, I can wear them too. I bet Miss Cindy (his bus driver) will say Oh my gosh I can't believe it!" When the bus came and Cindy opened the door, Jimmy held onto the rail and walked up the four steps. He stopped at the top and said, "Look! Look at my new shoes! And no braces!" Miss Cindy said, "Oh my gosh, I can't believe it." He turned to me and smiled. He got into his seat, blew me a kiss, and gave me the thumbs up sign like he always does.

I went back into the house thinking about how his teachers and friends would react, and wishing I could see and hear everything. The few hours he was gone I paced and wrote in my journal. I prepared snacks for his school party the next day. Chooch was decorating the house, the yard, and the mailbox for our big party the next night. I went outside to wait for the bus 15 minutes early. It was a beautiful day and I could hardly wait for him to come home. I feel this way every day he goes to school, but today when the bus turned the corner, I wanted to run down the street and meet him.

The bus pulled up and he still had that big smile on his face. He blew everyone kisses bye. We held hands and walked across the street into the driveway. He then stopped and said, "Mother this was my happiest day ever." As tears welled up in my eyes I bent down to hug him; he wrapped his arms around my neck and said, "I know, me too." We both cried as we hugged each other and seconds later laughed together. He told me how his friends liked his shoes and his teacher, Miss Susan, screamed when she saw them. I have a feeling she cried a little too.

Birthdays are always special, but this one is dear to my heart. I could have popped with pride looking at the smiles of Jimmy's grandparents, aunts, uncles, and cousins, watching him do some of the things we all hoped for, but were a little afraid to believe he could ever do.

He still wears his night braces and day braces without a fuss. I let him pick the days he wants to wear his new shoes. Jimmy is my joy, my strength, and the best of me. He verifies my belief in miracles and the power of love daily.

Letting go..., (See you at 3:00)
By Marie Kennedy

Sun is hot and we play all day
Fun started at the end of May
Planting a garden and watching it grow
Laying in the grass with the bugs aglow
Sleeping late and picnics for lunch
Hugs from my son, he loves me a bunch
Look Mother, a picture I painted for you
with orange flowers, green grass and sky of blue.
Oh wait, I must add a rainbow too!
I watch him paint his, eye brow up and tongue sticking out
"Helps me concentrate," he says with a smile and never a pout.
Starting all day school , I smile how can that be?
It seems just yesterday he was three.
He started school then, just a few hours a day
We miss him anytime he is away
The past three years he attended a special class
He wasn't always able to walk in the grass
He wears braces on his legs and he runs kinda slow
Will the other children be kind? I need to know.
This time he leaves early, won't be back until 3:00
I feel like a baby, now it's me not we.
That first day Dad will be there too
He always knows just what to do.
Our son is eager to go and meet new friends
I want him to grow and to learn and to blend
I worry a little as each mother would
I want to go with him, and that's no good
The time has come for letting go
He is ready, this I know.
This year he will attend regular class
20 children his age, he will have a blast
Also ready to ride the Big Bus
Eating lunch at school, not with us.
I don't want him to see the fear in my eyes
The ache in my heart and tremble inside
It's too late he already knows.
He hugs me tight before he goes
"Don't worry Mom, I'm a tough little guy"

89

The time has come to say good-bye
"I know" I say and hug him tight
"Don't worry about me, I'm alright"
Oh the tears I fight
New friends say hello as he sits in his seat.
A big-boy world he is ready to meet
warm hands on my shoulders to comfort me
"We love you honey, see you at 3:00"

Cerebral Palsy Information

Cerebral Palsy Connection (CPC)
www.cpconnection.com
(provides communication with other parents and many other helpful links)

United Cerebral Palsy
www.ucp.org
(in the US, type in your zip code and you will get the addresses of your nearest CP resources)

Empowering Caregivers
www.caregivers.com
(inspirational stories, chats, list of recommended reading)

Research Link
Barnes Jewish Children's Hospital
BJC/Human Performance Lab
http://roadrunner.carenet.org/
(Cp research lab..click Cerebral Palsy)

THE ANSWER SLEUTH'S CEREBRAL PALSY
http://www.answersleuth.com/health/diseases/cerebral_palsy.shtml
(definitions and over 100 links for additional CP info)

To get updates on Jimmy and see recent photographs
visit my website
www.mariekennedy.com

Marie Kennedy

Special Thanks

Tracy: You helped me turn a 17,000-word sentence into a story I am proud to call mine. I will always be grateful.

Family and friends: Your belief in me as a mother and while writing this book, encourages me every day. I know that I can always call on you and never feel alone.

Teachers, doctors, therapists, nurses, dentists, bus drivers, casting and braces personnel, and helpers: Your genuine concern and care for our son eased our fears and allowed us to make the right decisions for Jimmy. He looks forward to therapy and appointments like a social event, and that's because of you.

Chooch and Jimmy: Your love, support, and inspiration have enabled me to be honest and proud to share our story. I have everything I ever dreamed of—right here with you.

Marie Kennedy

A few words about *My Perfect Son...*

"I cannot tell you how much I enjoyed reading your thoughts and insights on raising such a beautiful child. I felt your book was very moving and would be cherished by other parents who have been blessed enough to be sent a child with special needs. I often tell people that my patients are my heroes. They are my spiritual leaders, gurus, and I think Jimmy is the true personification of those statements. Required reading for all my students."

—Dr. Chuck Dietzen, M.D. Physiatrist
Chief of Staff, St. Vincent Children's Specialty Hospital
Assistant Professor of Medicine, Indiana University Medical Center

"I thoroughly enjoyed your book about Jimmy and cerebral palsy. You've provided a much needed family perspective that many parents never receive... I especially enjoyed your creative ideas for home exercises along with the pictures...Your book provides a missing view about the personal life of a family with a child with C.P. Thanks for your wonderful contribution to C.P. literature."

—Sandy Ross MHS, PT, PCS, Senior Physical Therapist
Barnes Jewish and St. Louis Children's Hospitals
Dept. Of Rehabilitation at Washington University

"As a Mother, it brought tears to my eyes. I was moved by your honesty...As a therapist, I was very impressed with all the activities and adaptations you established. Everything was presented in a very thorough way, explaining how and why you did everything in terms that anyone could understand. This book is beneficial to parents and professionals alike."

—Sue Anderson, Physical Therapist

"Both my wife, who is a physician, and I were very moved by your story. I only wish I would have had the opportunity to read a book like this prior to doing Pediatrics in my medical school rotations or even residency. I will certainly recommend it to my colleagues and those medical students and nursing students who will follow in our footsteps."

—Dr. Robert Arthur, MD

"I would recommend this book to health care professionals, teachers, students, and parents. After reading this book, you will have a better understanding of C.P. And it will remind you to place the emphasis on the child not the disorder. I loved this book!"

—Jennifer Satterfield-Siegel, Pediatric Dentistry

95

"Your book provided us with exactly what we were looking for and with what we needed to hear. As my husband and I pored over it together, we found ourselves speaking out loud saying "yes" and "remember that." It described beautifully the mix of emotions from worry and concern to joy and elation that we feel daily. It gave us so many wonderful ideas of things we can do to help our son and inspired us to work harder...And the many encouraging photographs are wonderful."

—Jennifer T. Martinez, Mother

About the Author

Marie Kennedy is a wife, mother, motivational speaker, and freelance writer. She is published in numerous online magazines and has been a guest speaker at schools associated with the program "Everybody Counts." She has also been a speaker at hospitals, child advocacy conventions, and Universities, providing the human side of Cerebral Palsy to therapy and medical students.

Marie is a member of the NLAPW (National League of American Pen Women) and recently won a short story writing contest with *Jimmy's New Shoes*, which will be published in *Chicken Soup for the Mothers Soul 2*, available April 2001.

The Kennedy family was taped for a regional (state of Indiana and Louisville, Kentucky) PBS show, *Across Indiana* in May of 2000. The show has aired several times on PBS WFYI channel 20. For more information refer to show number 1028, WFYI website http://www.wfyi.org.

Marie welcomes emails and letters. She can be contacted through her website www.mariekennedy.com, Email MarieKennedy@aol.com, or write to Marie Kennedy PO box 71 Carmel, Indiana 46082-0071.